MAR **1 3** 2013

D0209237

A Note from David Macaulay

Dear reader,

When I was a kid I did not like to read. But if a book had pictures, I would try to read it. The pictures made reading more fun. They helped me understand what the words meant. Words and pictures are still my favorite way to read a story. They are also my favorite way to tell a story.

The castle in this story is like the ones I visited when I was young. They were built in a country called Wales. I grew up in England so we did not have to go far to see them. There are many kinds of castles in the world but these are still my favorites.

David Macaulay

Dear parents and teachers,

Beginning reader books, like the one you are holding, have long served as the portal through which children can be lured into the world of words. The most successful of these use illustration to support the hard work of learning to decode text. But children are not only learning verbal literacy, they are learning visual literacy as well. They learn to read pictures, to pick up clues that may help them infer meaning and add depth to the words.

All the topics chosen for the books in this series are nonfiction. Whether they are historical or contemporary, from the natural world or the manmade, the topics reflect things we know children are interested in and curious about. Since these books are intended to stimulate both verbal and visual literacy, information is conveyed in both art and text.

To support the reader's curiosity, at the back of the book there is a glossary, a list of suggested books and other media, and an index.

It is my hope that these books will connect future citizens with their increasingly complex planet in a meaningful and creative way. If I've done my job well, you will enjoy reading and looking, too.

David Macaulay

For activities and reading tips, visit myreadersonline.com.

DAVID MACAULAY STUDIO
An imprint of Roaring Brook Press/
Macmillan Children's Publishing Group

Copyright ©2012 by David Macaulay
All rights reserved.
Printed in China by Toppan Leefung Printing Ltd.,
Dongguan City, Guangdong Province
For information, address Macmillan Children's
Publishing Group, 175 Fifth Avenue,
New York, NY 10010.

Library of Congress Control Number: 2011962088

ISBN: 978-1-59643-744-9 (hardcover)
10 9 8 7 6 5 4 3 2 1
ISBN: 978-1-59643-766-1 (paperback)
10 9 8 7 6 5 4 3 2 1

First Edition: 2012

mackids.com

This is a Level 4 book
LEXILE 500L

DAVID MACAULAY

CASTLE
How It Works

with
SHEILA KEENAN

David Macaulay Studio
Macmillan Children's Publishing Group
New York

PUBLIC LIBRARY SAN MATEO, CALIFORNIA

The castle stands high
on a rocky hill.
It has tall towers,
thick stone walls,
doors of wood and iron,
and a wide moat.

There is *NO* welcome mat!

People cannot just walk into a castle.
The castle was built
to keep the people inside safe.
It keeps other people safely outside!

Are you *friend* or *foe*?

If you are a friend
you must first climb a steep ramp.
It ends at a wooden drawbridge.
The drawbridge crosses the moat.
You are now facing the outer wall.
It's called the outer curtain.

You walk toward the first gatehouse.
A tower stands on each side.
Guards decide who can come in.
They watch everyone *very* closely!
Welcome friend!

When you get past the guards
you are *still* not all the way in.
There is another wall in front of you
even taller than the outer curtain!
It's called the inner curtain.
It has an even bigger gatehouse.

You guessed it. More guards!
The inner curtain has a high tower
at each of its four corners.
Guards can see for miles
from the tops of these towers.
They can shoot in every direction.

At last! You are deep within the castle.
Welcome to the inner ward.
This courtyard is a lively place!
Horses are fed in the stable
below the barracks.
Soldiers are playing a game.
The blacksmith makes a new horseshoe.

The blacksmith's children are chasing chickens.
The cook builds a big fire in the kitchen.
The cook's helper draws water from the well.
He must water the garden.
The dog gets a drink, too.

The lord and lady live in one of the high towers.
The walls of these rooms are painted.
Fresh herbs are tossed on the floors.
This makes the rooms smell good.

A spiral staircase goes all the way to the roof.
Guards keep watch from the walls
and towers day and night.

The ground floor is filled with dried food
and barrels of wine and cider.
Beneath the ground floor is
the dark, damp dungeon.

The chapel is in another high tower.
The priest is one of the few people
in the castle who can read.

The roof above the chapel collects rainwater.
It flows through a pipe into a tank
and then all the way down to the kitchen sink.

A guard has stopped to use the toilet.
Listen! Can you hear his teeth chattering?
He sits over a hole
cut into a cold stone slab.
Below the hole is a shaft
that goes down to a pit.
The knight uses hay for toilet paper.

The largest building in the
inner ward is the great hall.
The great hall has fireplaces in the walls.
It has tall windows to let in light.
Servants arrange tables and benches.
They put out wooden bowls and
spoons, but no plates.
People will use thick slices
of stale bread for plates.
The great hall will soon
be ready for dinner.

If you are a foe, or an enemy,
you won't be let in.
To capture the castle
you will have to surround it and wait.
This is called a siege.
A siege stops supplies
from getting into the castle.

But you'd better be patient.
Remember all the dried food
in the towers?
And don't forget the water in the well.
Your army may surround the castle,
but the people inside can last
a long time.

Are you in a hurry?
You'll have to get past
the town wall first.
Bring on the battering ram!

The battering ram hangs by chains
inside a wooden shed.
You swing it back and forth.

It hits the wall hard!

If you make a big enough hole,
you can crawl through it.
Now you can open the gatehouse doors
and let your soldiers in.

But the soldiers inside
can see you coming.
Guards remove the supports
under the drawbridge.
One end flips up,
the other end drops down.
No more bridge!

You could wheel in a catapult.
It looks like a giant wooden spoon.
You can fire big heavy rocks.
You can also fire smelly,
germy dead animals.
Fire! *Whoosh!* Pigs away!

Perhaps you could build a ladder
to scale the outer curtain.
Wait until dark.
You might get as far as
the inner gatehouse.
But, *Slam!*

The portcullis crashes down behind you.
Heavy doors block the other end
of the passage.

You are trapped.
Guards above drop rocks and hot water
through "murder holes" in the ceiling.

If you do get through this gatehouse,
there are many more soldiers waiting.
They patrol the battlements along the tops
of all the walls and towers.
Archers will greet you with flaming arrows.

It is no use.
Your men are brave and willing to fight,
but in the end you must give up.
You did your best,
but the castle is too strong.
The dungeon is now full.
The rest of your army
disappears into the woods.

Slowly, the inner ward comes back to life.
The mess will be cleaned up tomorrow.
Tonight there will be a celebration.
The cook has put away his bow and arrows
and grabbed a spoon.
Bring on the meat, beans, onions, and puddings.
And please don't forget the eel pie!

29

Words To Know

archer someone who shoots with a bow and arrow or crossbow

barracks a building where soldiers live

battering ram a heavy wooden beam or log that is rammed against enemy walls

battlement the top of a castle wall

blacksmith someone who makes and fits horseshoes and mends things made of iron

catapult a weapon used for firing things over castle walls

drawbridge a bridge than can be raised and lowered

dungeon an underground prison

foe an enemy

gatehouse a fortified entryway often protected by a portcullis

inner curtain the high wall around the inner ward

inner ward the castle courtyard

moat a deep ditch

outer curtain the lower wall around the outer part of the castle

portcullis a heavy grille or gate to close off a gatehouse

siege surrounding a castle to make those inside surrender

spiral a pattern that winds around in circles

To Learn More

Built To Last by David Macaulay. Houghton Mifflin Harcourt, 2010.
Castles by Stephanie Turnbull, illustrated by Colin King. Usborne, 2007.

Castle (DVD), hosted by David Macaulay, PBS Home Video, 2006.

www.castles.org
This site shows castles from all over the world.
There is a link to children's pages. There is also a list of castles for sale!

http://www.neuschwanstein.de
Click the second flag from the left for English.
The Sleeping Beauty castle in Disneyland was inspired by this real castle in Germany!
The site also has a children's page with games.

Index